Teenage Refugees From

NICARAGUA

Speak Out

IN THEIR OWN VOICES

Teenage Refugees From

NICARAGUA

Speak Out

K. MELISSA CERAR

M012165189

ROSEN PUBLISHING GROUP, INC.
NEW YORK

Published in 1995 by The Rosen Publishing Group, Inc.
29 East 21st Street, New York, NY 10010

First Edition
Copyright © 1995 by The Rosen Publishing Group, Inc.

Manufactured in the United States of America.

Library of Congress Cataloging-in-Publication Data

Teenage refugees from Nicaragua speak out / [edited by] K. Melissa Cerar. —
1st ed.
　　p.　　cm. — (In their own voices)
　Includes bibliographical references and index.
　ISBN 0-8239-1849-7
　1. Nicaraguan American teenagers—Juvenile literature. 2. Refugees—United
States—Juvenile literature. I. Cerar, K. Melissa. II. Series.
E184.N53T44 1995
973'.04687285—dc20　　　　　　　　　　　　　94-40665
　　　　　　　　　　　　　　　　　　　　　　　　　CIP
　　　　　　　　　　　　　　　　　　　　　　　　　AC

Contents

Plagued by civil unrest, Nicaragua has been the site of many protests. Here the United National Opposition demonstrators burn a Sandinista flag.

INTRODUCTION

Immigrants arrive daily in the United States from all the countries of Latin America. In addition to the quarter million legal immigrants, an unknown number enter illegally every year. Estimates of Latin American immigrants range from less than 100,000 to more than 500,000. Recently, the majority have come from Nicaragua and El Salvador because of war and economic crises in those countries.

Nicaragua is bordered by Costa Rica to the south and El Salvador and Honduras to the north. To the east is the Caribbean Sea, and to the west, the Pacific Ocean. Although the country is rich in natural resources, it is racked by poverty and unrest. This pattern of trouble was established early in its history, which has been notable for violence.

MAS VALE PÁJARO
EN MANO, QUE VER
UN CIENTO VOLAR.

ENGLISH TRANSLATION FROM SPANISH:
It is better to have one bird in hand,
than to have a hundred birds fly by.

Pre-Columbian Nicaragua was influenced by the Maya and Chibcha people. Today, as then, the Miskito people inhabit the Atlantic coast, a narrow strip skirting the Caribbean.

The territory was conquered by the Spanish in 1552 and remained under their rule until 1821, after which it was united for a time with Mexico. In 1823, Nicaragua became a part of the United Provinces of Central America. When the federation was dissolved in 1838, Nicaragua became an independent republic.

For more than fifty years the country was divided into two political groups, the Liberals, based in

Conflict between the people and the government continues today as students fight to keep their antigovernment banner while police fight to confiscate it.

León, and the Conservatives, based in Granada. The groups fought brutally for control as power shifted back and forth. In 1855 the Liberals invited William Walker, an American adventurer with a small band of followers, to join their cause. He managed to capture and sack Granada, and in the following year he became president. His seizure of properties aroused Conservative anger, however, and in 1857 he was forced out of office and fled the country.

The Conservatives then remained in control for more than thirty years, until in 1893 a revolution

9

Anastasio Somoza DeBayle was named president after his brother, Luis, and father, Anastasio García, had held the office. He was also head of the brutal National Guard.

brought the Liberal leader José Santos Zelaya to the presidency. He ruled as a dictator for the next seventeen years.

Adolfo Díaz, elected provisional president in 1910, faced serious civil unrest. He appealed to the United States for support, and a small force of Marines was sent in 1912 and later reinforced. Under a treaty of 1916, the U.S. paid Nicaragua $3,000,000 for the right to build a canal across the country and to establish a naval base. This agreement aroused resentment and led to anti-American guerrilla warfare in Nicaragua. In 1925 the Marines were withdrawn, and the civil war grew more intense. One man who sought an independent Nicaragua, General César Augusto Sandino, put together an army of 3,000 men and successfully resisted the second U.S.-backed occupation for six years (1926–33). Sandino agreed to a cease-fire when the last Marine left the country. He kept his promise but was assassinated in 1933 by U.S.-backed Anastasio Somoza García, who began a brutal and corrupt four-year dictatorship supported by the U.S. and the Nicaraguan National Guard.

The National Guard was commanded by Somoza, who had been trained by the Marines. It was the tool he used to build the wealthy Somoza dynasty. The Guard was utterly corrupt. It ran a vast system of illegal activity including prostitution and gambling. By the end of the Somoza rule, the Nicaraguan National Guard was more skilled in U.S. military tactics than any country in Latin America.

Nicaragua sustained relations with the U.S. by catering politically and socially to diplomats and politicians. Somoza was succeeded by his son, Luis Somoza Debayle, who was followed by his brother, Anastasio Somoza DeBayle, a West Point graduate. Anastasio outlawed all trade unions and banned all opposition, killing members of the peasant movement for freedom.

In the 1960s, the Sandinist National Liberation Front (SNLF) was organized. Named for Sandino, it developed anti-Somoza guerrilla warfare that lasted for seventeen years. It also sought to redistribute the wealth of the rich among the overwhelmig majority, the poor. Martial law was imposed in 1974 after Sandinista guerrillas kidnapped officials. In 1977, Roman Catholic bishops charged the government with mistreating civilians in its anti-guerrilla campaign. Violent opposition to the government spread throughout the country. In 1978 Pedro Joaquín Chamorro, editor of the newspaper *La Prensa*, was assassinated for his anti-governmental views. Strikes and protests were widespread. In May 1979, Sandinista guerrillas invaded Nicaragua and touched off a seven-week offensive. In July 1979 Somoza fled Nicaragua.

Reconstruction of the economy began immediately after the Sandinista Revolution. Somoza's lands—40 percent of the country's economic resources, were nationalized. The Sandinista

Former President Anastasio Somoza DeBayle, center, was forced to flee Nicaragua in 1979, ending a devastating four-decade regime.

Former President Daniel Ortega was a key leader in the Sandinista government.

Popular Army replaced the National Guard. A literacy campaign was initiated, as were health programs.

In 1981, U.S. President Ronald Reagan announced his plans to destroy the Marxist Sandinistas. In 1982, U.S.-supported former National Guardsmen invaded Nicaragua from Honduras. In 1983, Reagan admitted having provided secret funds for covert CIA operations against Nicaragua and having aided counterrevolutionaries called *contras*. Reagan called the *contras* "freedom fighters." In 1984, Nicaragua accused the U.S. of mining its ports. The International Court of Justice agreed and ordered the U.S. to stop mining and cease aiding attacks on Nicaragua's territory.

With the possibility of a Central American war, the governments of Colombia, Mexico, Panama, and Venezuela began to negotiate a settlement to the conflict. Ministers advanced peace plans to prevent an invasion by U.S. troops.

Contra attacks increased with support from the U.S. General elections were held in Nicaragua in November 1984. Many parties were represented, the Sandinista Government being the most widely supported with 67 percent of the vote. In 1985 Reagan declared a trade embargo against Nicaragua.

In 1987, a new Nicaraguan constitution instituted a presidential system whereby a president would be elected to a six-year term by direct vote. Legislators would be represented proportionally to districts. Also in that year, the United Nations and the

Members of the *contra* guerrilla forces had to rely on food they found in the wild, such as bananas and wild turkeys, to supplement their daily rations of rice and beans. Some of the more remote camps were a thirty-day walk from provision centers.

The *contra* forces were made up of guerrillas from Nicaragua's neighbors, Honduras and Guatemala, as well as native Nicaraguans.

Organization of American States met with the Central American leaders to negotiate in Esquipulas, Guatemala. This meeting called for an end to outside support for armed opposition groups and the opening of communications—mediated by the Catholic Church—within each of the countries. *Contras* who put down their arms were promised amnesty and representation in the government.

A Commission for Reconciliation was formed in Nicaragua immediately. Censorship of the media was lifted, and *La Prensa* resumed publication. An almost across-the-board cease-fire went into effect in Nicaragua although *contra* leaders said they

17

The various wars throughout Nicaragua's history have forced many families to pack up
their belongings and search for a safer place to live.

The lives of many Nicaraguans, such as this family, were irrevocably changed by the various wars throughout Nicaragua's history.

would continue to fight.

Beginning in 1988, inflation increased dramatically. The U.S. Ambasador to Nicaragua was accused of supporting anti-Sandinista activities and was forced to leave the country. In turn, the Nicaraguan Ambassador to the U.S. was asked to leave.

The agreements made at Esquipulas seemed to lose ground quickly. President Daniel Ortega began fresh talks with the five Central American presidents in Costa del Sol, El Salvador. The Sandinistas proposed to move elections up to February 1990 and to accept modifications to the electoral law under

19

Small merchants and farmers protest that the national subsidies proposed for them by the Nicaraguan government are not enough to sustain their operations through the acute economic crisis.

one condition—that the *contras* remove their forces based in Honduras within three months of the signing of the agreement. But the U.S. insisted that the *contras* continue in Honduras, and Vice President George Bush persuaded Congress to give them $40 million in "humanitarian aid."

Between 1981 and 1990 the United States covertly and then openly supported *contra* rebels fighting the Sandinistas in a civil war that devastated the country both economically and morally.

In the 1990 presidential vote, Ortega represented the Sandinistas and Violeta Barrios de Chamorro,

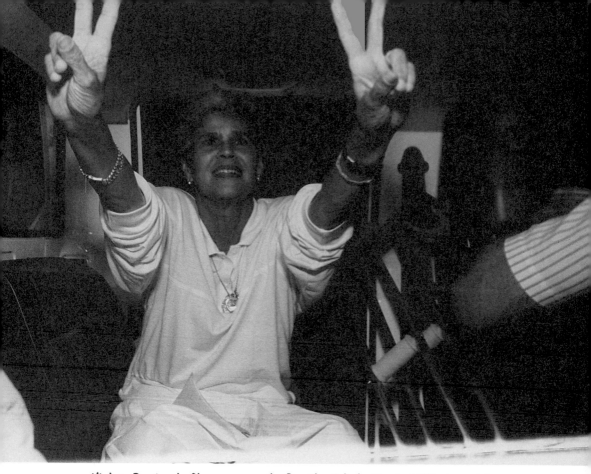

Violeta Barrios de Chamorro won the Presidential election in 1990, in part by promising to come to a compromise between the Sandinista government and the *contras.*

the widow of Pedro Joaquín Chamorro, represented the National Opposition Union (UNO). The U.S. supported Mrs. Chamorro and made it clear that U.S. support for the *contra* war would stop if she did win. Although the polls predicted a Sandinista victory, Ms. Chamorro won the vote by a landslide.

Before taking office on April 25, Chamorro signed an agreement with the Sandinistas recognizing the standing constitution and the achievements of the revolution and also supporting disarmament of the *contras.* Chamorro took charge of defense and retained General Humberto Ortega as comman-

21

This eleven-year-old boy claims to have been fighting the Sandinista army for three years.

der of the armed forces. In addition, compulsory army service was abolished. Vice President Virgilio Godoy and other members of Chamorro's staff withdrew from office, saying she had not kept her campaign promises.

With the new government in place, things seemed to be taking a positive turn. But workers became restless, eventually striking for higher wages. Eventually a compromise was reached. Some former *contra* leaders banded together to form the Party of Nicaraguan Resistance. They denounced the actions of *contra* leaders who had recently resumed their violent attacks in the north.

In 1991 President Chamorro made agreements with the Sandinista leadership. In 1992, negotiations were resumed between the Chamorro government, the Sandinistas, the armed forces, armed pro-Sandinista civilians, and the *contras.*

Although there is a shaky peace in the new regime, rumbles of dissatisfaction are still heard among laborers, former *contras* bitter about continued Sandinista control of the army and the police, and finally the business community, discouraged by the slow recovery of the economy.

*   *   *

Some of the teenagers interviewed for this book asked that their photographs not be used. In most cases, they have done so to protect relatives still in Nicaragua. They fear that their families may be in danger if their identities are discovered. In all cases, we haved used only the students' first names in order to protect their privacy.◆

Iris came to the United States at the age of fourteen. She now lives in Far Rockaway, New York. She is sensitive, funny, and happily living with her family in the United States.

IRIS
THEN THE SANDINISTAS CAME

I am from San Carlos Rio San Juan, in Nicaragua. It is a small town near the border of Costa Rica. I have three brothers and one sister.

We had a good life there. My family was happy. We owned a restaurant. Then the Sandinistas came. It was difficult to get supplies. We would have supplies for maybe a week and then run out. They started rationing supplies so we would get two pounds of rice for a week, two pounds of beans, a little bit of ham. For my family that is not so much, not enough. The Sandinistas took our containers for milk so we couldn't get more. Finally we had to leave.

My mom came to the States first. She stayed for a year, then came back to get us. My brother was just a baby then. We had milk for a while, but then we stopped getting milk. The baby was just drinking water. He was sick.

We took a plane to Tijuana, Mexico. We stayed in a motel there for two days until someone came to guide us across the *puente* (bridge). We went all the way on foot, and ended up in Los Angeles, California.

I went to school for one week in California. Then we came to New York, because we have family here.

I like the United States. It is nice here. My English is still really bad. I even went to a bilingual school, but as you see, it didn't help. Everyone here speaks Spanish, so I never really had to learn. My brothers and sisters, they all speak English very well.

Growing up now in Nicaragua is still difficult, but there is less struggle than when I was there. I went home two years ago. All the children are barefoot. Everyone is really poor. I don't have a desire to go back there to live. People are very poor, but now people really just come here to be with their families and see if they can make money. There are jobs here for us.

I am still adjusting to North American culture. It is very different. Sometimes I feel lonely, but not enough to go back to Nicaragua. We cook Nicaraguan food: *arroz con pollo* (chicken and rice), *yucca* (a potato-like vegetable), *chicharon* (fried pork skins), and *vigoron*, which is made with *yucca*, *chicharon*, and chopped cabbage with

Food is in short supply at refugee centers throughout Nicaragua. People consider themselves lucky if they get rice and beans for breakfast, lunch, and dinner.

Even while resting, *contras* were always armed and ready to fight.

lemon or vinegar and salt.

It is hard being in the United States, even though it is better than Nicaragua. I work at a dry cleaner's— work, work, work all the time with no vacations. I keep up very seldom with events back at home unless there is something really big happening.◆

Manuel grew up in Granada, in the southwest of Nicaragua. He lives in New York with his family. He is creative, intelligent, and soft-spoken. He found it difficult to adjust to the new culture he found in the United States.

MANUEL
CROSSING THE BORDER

I grew up in Granada. My family owns a market there, like the Chinese groceries here.

I came to the United States because of the war. I was twelve years old. They were recruiting fourteen-year-old kids for the war. My family wanted to keep me safe from that, so they sent me here. I was a "wetback," which is slang for someone who swam across the Rio Grande to the United States.

I came through Mexico. A guy had to bring me across. I remember that we had to hide in a small house in Mexico. It was a motel or something. We ran a mile and a half. Then we had to cross the border. There was this big wide road and all these cars going by. I was terrified. There were fifty of us running and trying not to get caught. It was so scary, all of us running around like that, trying to hide from the police. I didn't know really what was going on or where I was going.

The Sandinista armed forces recruited students to fight the war against the *contras*. This soldier is teaching high school freshmen in Managua how to use a rocket launcher.

A guy brought us across the border in the trunk of his car. They wanted to put me in first, because I was the youngest and the smallest, but I said no way because I was so small. There were all these fat guys, I mean really fat, and I didn't want to get squashed. So I finally got to go on top. But I remember so clearly not being able to breathe. My family had to pay $1,000 to get someone to take me across the border.

I first went to California, then to Miami. I was in Miami for a year, where I lived with an aunt and went to school. I faced discrimination not because

I was Latin American, but because I was the new guy. The other kids made fun of me because I couldn't speak English. They called me stupid, but I was really shy, so it was difficult for me. The kids wanted to beat me up.

I still see discrimination at work. It's not at me, but at a new guy at work. My boss always calls him stupid because he doesn't speak English. I get really angry because I remember what it feels like. I get into trouble if I say anything.

It took me about two years to learn English. It made my studies difficult. I am still adjusting to society here. I don't understand why people are so concerned with the color of people's skin. My dad is black, my mom is white. I am brown. In Nicaragua, there are all different colors of people, black, brown, yellow, white. It doesn't matter. Here it's such a big problem.◆

Julissa lives in Washington, D.C., with her cousins and her aunt. She is reserved and quiet. Active in her church, she also enjoys hanging out with her friends. She has had trouble adjusting to life in the United States but is doing well, having carved a niche for herself in her Spanish-speaking community. Julissa hopes that the rest of her family will soon join her here in the United States.

JULISSA
LEARNING ENGLISH

I was sixteen when I left Nicaragua. I come from a family of nine children. I am from León. It's a pretty large town. My family left because some of our relatives had already left. We are a big family. They left because of the war. The war has been going on for about twelve years. We came by plane into Baltimore.

It was scary when we first came. It's very different in the States. I miss my friends at home. My mother is at home still. I miss her very much. Now I am living with cousins. My sisters and brothers will come later.

School is different in Nicaragua. It starts at 7:30 in the morning. You get out at 12 or 12:30. We go home for lunch. After school we do the same kinds   **35** of things the kids do there, hang out, play games and stuff. In that way it's not so different from high school here.

When I got here I didn't know English. I had to learn it. That was very difficult. I don't speak English very well. I started feeling comfortable after about two years when I could speak better. We speak Spanish at home here. We also eat Nicaraguan food. *Corchata* is one of the things we eat. My grandma makes it for us. We eat tacos and burritos. They are similar to the Mexican version.

I want to go to Nicaragua and see my mother and my family. I don't know about politics. It is difficult to live there now for people our age. It is hard to make money. All the young men had to join the military and fight in the war. Many died. Most of the people I know that went died. You are supposed to be eighteen to fight, but it wasn't a choice. Even if you didn't want to, you had to go. They changed that though. It's different now. It is very expensive to live in Nicaragua. It is easier to get a job here in the States. It is so difficult there to get a job.◆

Many refugees from Nicaragua were set up in camps that housed more people than they were built to accommodate.

Fernando, sixteen, lives with his stepfather and his mother. He is popular and has a good sense of humor. He likes living in the United States. Like American kids, he spends his time hanging out with friends, going to the movies, and having an occasional slice of pizza.

FERNANDO
THEY JUST GIVE YOU A GUN

I was born in Managua. I came to the United States when I was six years old.

I lived with my grandma in Nicaragua because my mother came to the States first. My mother came illegally. She swam across a river to Mexico. She was what people call a "wetback." A guy gave her a ride from Mexico, and then she went to Miami, then to Washington.

My mom sent for me. I came on a plane with my grandmother. My uncle, who worked for the U.S. embassy in Nicaragua, gave me a visa. He pretended he was my father so I could come to the United States to be with my mom.

I don't have very much family here, just my mom, two uncles and an aunt, and my grandma. **39**

Life here is so easy compared to Nicaragua. There you have to work if you don't go to school. The reason my mom brought me out of Nicaragua was because of the war. There, when you are twelve or thirteen, they just give you a gun. You have to fight, and if you don't, they come get you. I know, because I had a cousin who was seventeen. He didn't want to fight, and every day the soldiers came to the door and beat him up until he agreed to go. I remember that so well.

Adjusting to life here wasn't so hard. I was in the third grade. I remember when I first got to school I was the only Spanish-speaking person, so people used to pick on me. They called me names like Mexican Burrito. They always called me Mexican as if everyone is Mexican. It made me laugh, but it made me feel really bad too. Now things are fine. All my friends are *Nicas* (young Nicaraguans) or from El Salvador or Guatemala. We all just have fun and hang out.

I miss my cousins at home. I went to visit two years ago, and it was really fun. I had a good time. I still keep in touch with people from there. The people are really poor. When I went, there was a strike going on. There was a lot less food than usual. My little cousin was almost starving. We all had to share the food.

My cousins told me that it's dangerous there now. There are all these gangs. Each *barrio* (neighborhood) in Managua has a different gang, a lot like here. Only those gangs are a lot more

During the battle between Somoza's National Guard and the SNLF in the late 1970s, people fled Managua any way they could to escape the gunfire and violence.

dangerous. If you were wearing a pair of cheap shoes from the United States, like $10.99 shoes, they would kill you for those shoes. You can hear the people screaming in the streets. It's not safe to go out after 3:00 in the afternoon.

Here I've had some jobs after school. I worked at Sears, then a restaurant, then Woody's (Woodward & Lothrop), Hecht's, and a store called Up Against the Wall. I try to help my mom out. Usually she says no, keep your money, so I use it to get my own clothes and stuff. After school we have to do homework before we go out. We eat Nicaraguan

41

The war between the contras and the Sandinistas destroyed many towns, including this town, Esteli.

food at home. One of the things my mom makes is *indio viejo*. It is a heavy sauce with hot peppers and it can be made with any kind of meat like chicken, pork, beef, or lamb.

I like the States now. I don't think I would want to go back to Nicaragua. It's too scary there now.◆

Claudia is a shy girl, soft-spoken and intelligent. She lives with her parents in Montebello, California.

Claudia was quite young when she came to the United States, but she has many memories. She does the same things here that occupied her time at home in Nicaragua—plays games with her friends, watches television, and, of course, does chores. Claudia would someday like to return to her native country.

CLAUDIA
GETTING USED TO THE U.S.

There are four in my family. I have one little sister. Both of my parents are here with us in the U.S. My grandma came to the United States a long time ago. After the war, my dad wanted to come here to be with my grandma. We flew from Managua, which is the capital of Nicaragua. That is where my family lived before. I was only six years old then, but I remember a little bit about Nicaragua.

I go to school here. Nobody does work here in school. You know how all the kids watch TV here? In Nicaragua, nobody plays unless they finish their chores: washing the clothes, taking care of the babies, doing dishes. And everyone wears uniforms in school. I was in second grade when I came here. I learned English and how to read at the same time. I think school here is easier.

Open markets are a common feature in Managua.

It took me two years to get used to the United States. It is fun to be here. I have friends and I like school, but I want to go back home someday. I have a lot of cousins and friends left in Nicaragua. My other grandma is still there. What is keeping us from going back home? Money. Money and jobs. There are no jobs in Nicaragua. Not like here. We went home to visit four years ago.

We speak Spanish at home. And we eat Nicaraguan food like *gallopinto*, which is rice and beans, and *tamales*.

There are no riches in Nicaragua. People are poor. Not like here. There is a lot of money in the United States. I guess what I would tell kids in the United States is that there is lots of suffering in Nicaragua, and no money. Life is easy here.◆

Mario lives in Miami with his mother and father. He attends the University of Miami, where he plays soccer. He works as a math, physics, and chemistry tutor four times a week at Miami Dade Community College. He also works at the Miami *Herald* putting together the classified ads. He hopes to gain political asylum in the United States.

MARIO
HIDING FROM THE MILITARY

I grew up in Managua, the capital of Nicaragua. I had to study in Masaya, a town about 12 miles from Managua. I went to a private school because the Sandinistas came and my father was against them. When you went to school they knew everything about you—how many members were in your family, where you lived. They made you learn their anthem and join their organizations. So I went to the private school where no one knew me.

The Sandinistas forced young men into the military, anyone between the ages of twelve and thirty. I was hiding from the military too.

In Nicaragua, there are only eleven grades. After the eleventh grade, you go to the university. To get my diploma from high school, I would have had to join the army voluntarily. Since I wouldn't

Both the Sandinistas and the *contra* guerrillas involved children and the elderly in fighting their battles. Pictured here are a 78-year-old man, who calls himself the "oldest *contra*," and a fourteen-year-old boy.

Thousands of people were forced to flee their homes as the National Guard fought the Sandinista guerrillas. This young boy rides to safety on his sister's shoulders.

do it, I lost credit for my last year in high school in Nicaragua.

I was sixteen when we left Nicaragua. It was in November. My father left before me. I was to meet him in Guatemala. They were trying to kill him so he went to Honduras.

I went to a Catholic school, so a priest from the school told the embassy that I was going to the seminary. I got a transit visa for thirty days to Honduras. I could not take a plane so I took a bus to Las Manos, Nueva Segovia. It's northeast of Managua.

51

Thousands of people and street vendors gather in front of the Cathedral of the
Immaculate Conception of Mary, Managua.

From there I went to Chiquimullila, Guatemala. I
had no problem crossing the border. I met my
father in Guatemala City. We stayed for a week to
save a bit more money. My father had been there a
month, and I had $200 with me. We decided to go
on to the United States.

We got on a bus and the conductor asked us
for money. He could tell we were not from Mexico.
We gave him a lot of money, I don't remember
how much. When we crossed the border into
Mexico, he told the police there was no one on
board. They work together with the police, I am
sure. The economy is so poor, they will do anything

for money. We got off in Matías Romero, Oaxaca, Mexico. We were afraid to stay in a hotel, so we slept at the bus station. In the morning we went to the train station. We asked this guy to help us out, so he put us on the first car of a train in this little space. Then he stole everything we owned— clothing, money, everything. We had only the clothes on our backs. Thank God my father had told me not to put my passport in my bag. I had it hidden in my underwear, so I still had it.

After seven hours on the train, at 2 a.m., they made us jump, with the train still moving. We walked along the tracks until we came to a church, where they gave us food and money. A priest took us to another church to spend the night. We walked all the next day and came to a Catholic school, where the nuns allowed us to stay and work for a week, gardening and cleaning, to make money. From there we got to Vera Cruz. At a church there called La Gian Madre de Dios, a group of young people worked to help immigrants. They gave us clothes, money, and a third-class ticket to Mexico City. From there we went to Monterey and then on to Matamoros, the city closest to the Texas border. We waited until after Christmas, December 28th, to cross. We had been in Mexico for one month.

That morning, we walked until we found a remote place to cross the river. We crossed into Brownsville, Texas. We went to a place where the nuns help illegals. There we waited for my mom, who was to meet us. Once she arrived, we went

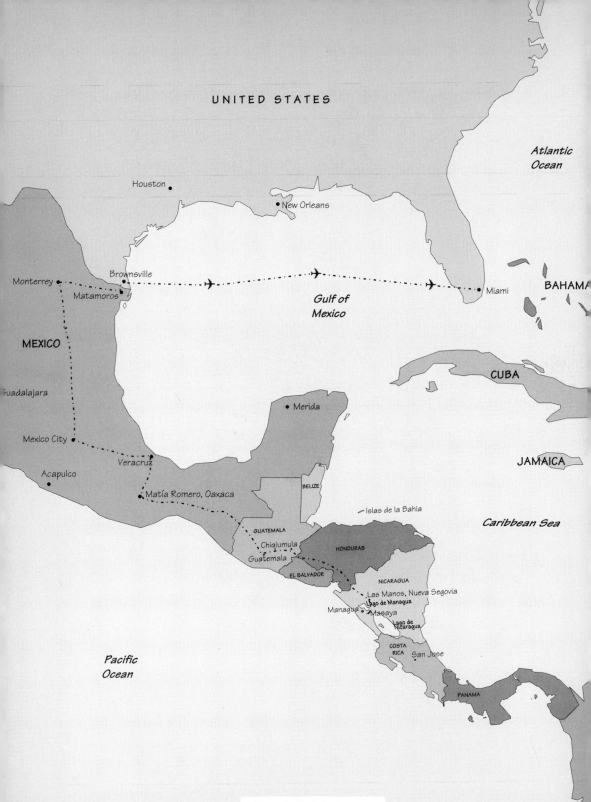

UNITED STATES

Atlantic
Ocean

Houston .

. New Orleans

BAHAMA

Monterrey .

Brownsville

Matamoros

. Miami

Gulf of
Mexico

MEXICO

CUBA

Guadalajara

Merida

Mexico City .

JAMAICA

Acapulco

Veracruz

Matía Romero, Oaxaca

BELIZE

Islas de la Bahia

Caribbean Sea

GUATEMALA

Chiqumula

HONDURAS

Guatemala

EL SALVADOR

NICARAGUA

Las Manos, Nueva Segovia

Lago de Managua

Managua . Masaya

Pacific
Ocean

Lago de
Nicaragua

COSTA
RICA

San Jose

PANAMA

Map of Mario's journey.

This rally was held after Daniel Ortega lost the 1990 Presidential elections, despite the Sandinistas' popularity.

together to Immigration and turned ourselves in. We asked for asylum. They were shocked, because no one *ever* does that. They asked us if we had family in the United States. My uncle lived in Miami, so they called him. He said he would take us in, so they let us go to Miami on January 12, 1989.

I wanted to go to school. It took about two months to get everything straightened out. I entered high school in my junior year at South Miami Senior High School.

I learned English from TV. I watched cartoons and listened to the radio. I took English as a

If support for the former Sandinista government was strong, so was the foothold of the *contras*. *Contra* guerrillas were still armed and supported by the United States as late as 1990.

second language (ESL) classes my junior year and the following summer.

At first they put me in the lowest math class. They thought because I didn't speak English I couldn't do it. Well, I took a test and I passed. I made the National Honor Society in Spanish and math. I was in the Junior Engineering Technical Society. I was on the math team and competed. I have three trophies from that. I also played soccer. I graduated eighteenth in my class with a 3.96 grade point average. I worked hard.

At first it was difficult to adjust. People are very materialistic in the U.S. I was starting from zero. I had nothing. They made fun of my clothes. They treated me differently. They pushed me out of their circle. Luckily, I met a friend from school back home who had been in the U.S. eight years. He took care of me.

My school was 50 percent white and 50 percent black and Hispanic. Some of the students were always telling the immigrants to go home, that we didn't belong here.

School is much easier in the U.S. In Nicaragua everyone takes the same courses at the same time. If you fail one subject, you go back a year for all subjects. In the U.S. you can fail one, two, or three classes, it seems, and still advance.

I've never been back to Nicaragua because of my political status. In my heart, I would love to return someday, but in reality, I know I will not. I am beginning to grow used to the United States. I know all the history. I feel secure here. If you don't agree with the government here, you have the freedom to say so. In my country, they kill you. If you work hard here, you can succeed. In my country, you work hard and never succeed. If you make money, they take it from you.

I have seven sisters and one brother. They are all there with my grandmother. We get letters and phone calls. They tell me that the Sandinistas are in power even though Chamorro was elected. She doesn't do anything.

When she came to power, the U.S. government sent lots of us home. Those kids who went home formed gangs. Drugs are really bad in Nicaragua: cocaine, marijuana, kids sniffing glue, gasoline, anything they can gets their hands on. It's to forget their hunger, their problems. That's one reason I don't want to go back.

My country is the greatest country I've ever lived in. There is a sense of unity. People care more about the spirit, the nonmaterial than the material things. If you want to become someone, set a goal, put it by your bed, and look at it every night. Work hard until you reach it for yourself and for your family.◆

Glossary

asylum Place where one is safe and secure.

barrio In Spanish-speaking countries, a suburb of a city; in the U.S., a Spanish-speaking neighborhood.

contra Short for counterrevolutionary, a member of any of the groups looking to overthrow the Sandinista government.

covert Concealed, hidden, disguised.

dictator Ruler with absolute power and authority.

discriminate To make a distinction in favor of or against on a categorical basis rather than according to merit.

dynasty Period of time during which a certain family reigns.

embargo Restriction or restraint of trade.

embassy Person or group sent as an official mission to a foreign government.

guerrilla Any member of a small defensive force

of volunteer soldiers, making surprise raids.

immigrant Person who has recently come to a location from another country.

Nicas Name young Nicaraguans use to refer to themselves.

puente Bridge.

ration Fixed portion.

union Organization uniting various individuals such as political units.

visa Endorsement on a passport showing that it has been examined by the proper authorities.

wetback Slang term referring to illegal aliens who swim across the Rio Grande from Mexico to the United States.

For Further Reading

Aldaraca, Bridget; Edward Baker; Ileana Rodriguez; and Marc Zimmerman. *Nicaragua in Revolution: The Poets Speak. Studies in Marxism*, Vol. V. Minneapolis: Anthropology Department, University of Minnesota, 1980.

Black, George. *Triumph of the People: The Sandinista Revolution in Nicaragua*. London: Zed Press, 1981.

Booth, John, and Walker, Thomas. *Understanding Central America*. Boulder, CO: Westview Press, 1993.

Booth, John A. *The End of the Beginning: The Nicaraguan Revolution*. Boulder, CO: Westview Press, 1981.

Borge, Tomás; Carlos Fonseca; Daniel Ortega, Humberto Ortega; and Jaime Wheelock. *Sandinistas Speak*. New York: Pathfinder Press, 1982.

Chavez, Linda. *Out of the Barrio: Toward a New Politics of Hispanic Assimilation.* New York: Basic Books, 1991.

Ellman, Richard. *Cocktails at Somozas: A Reporter's Sketchbook of Events in Revolutionary Nicaragua.* Cambridge, MA: Applewood Books, 1981.

Meiselas, Susan. *Nicaragua* (photography). New York: Pantheon Books, 1981.

Millett, Richard. *The Guardians of the Dynasty: A History of the U.S.-Created Guardia Nacional de Nicaragua and the Somoza Family.* Maryknoll, NY: Orbis 1977.

Randall, Margaret. *Sandino's Daughters.* Trumansberg, NY: Crossing Press, 1981.

Siems, Larry. *Between the Lines: Letters between Undocumented Mexican and Central American Immigrants and Their Families and Friends.* New York: The Ecco Press, 1992.

Stanford Central America Action Network. *Revolution in Central America.* Boulder, CO: Westview Press, 1983.

Weissberg, Arnold. *Nicaragua: An Introduction to the Sandinista Revolution.* New York: Pathfinder Press, 1981.

Index

ACKNOWLEDGMENTS
I would like to acknowledge the many people who helped me put together this book, especially Nora Brinto at Paternidad Nicaraguences, Max Ocón in California, Amnesty International, and the many groups nationwide that are working together to help immigrants from Latin America begin a new life.

ABOUT THE AUTHOR
K. Melissa Cerar is an artist and freelance writer. She currently lives in New Mexico.

PHOTO CREDITS
AP/Wide World Photos

DESIGN
Kim Sonsky